A Beginning-to-Read Book

# Being Kind to Yourself

by Mary Lindeen

NORWOOD HOUSE PRESS

**DEAR CAREGIVER,** The *Beginning to Read—Read and Discover* books provide emergent readers the opportunity to explore the world through nonfiction while building early reading skills. The text integrates both common sight words and content vocabulary. These key words are featured on lists provided at the back of the book to help your child expand his or her sight word recognition, which helps build reading fluency. The content words expand vocabulary and support comprehension.

Nonfiction text is any text that is factual. The Common Core State Standards call for an increase in the amount of informational text reading among students. The Standards aim to promote college and career readiness among students. Preparation for college and career endeavors requires proficiency in reading complex informational texts in a variety of content areas. You can help your child build a foundation by introducing nonfiction early. To further support the CCSS, you will find Reading Reinforcement activities at the back of the book that are aligned to these Standards.

Above all, the most important part of the reading experience is to have fun and enjoy it!

Sincerely,

*Shannon Cannon*

Shannon Cannon, Ph.D.
Literacy Consultant

Norwood House Press

For more information about Norwood House Press please visit our website at www.norwoodhousepress.com or call 866-565-2900.
© 2021 Norwood House Press. Beginning-to-Read™ is a trademark of Norwood House Press. All rights reserved. No part of this book may be reproduced or utilized in any form or by any means without written permission from the publisher.

Editor: Judy Kentor Schmauss
Designer: Sara Radka

**Photo Credits:**
Getty Images, cover, 3-29; Shutterstock, 1

**Library of Congress Cataloging-in-Publication Data**
Names: Lindeen, Mary, author.
Title: Being kind to yourself / by Mary Lindeen.
Description: [Chicago] : Norwood House Press, [2021] | Series: A beginning-to-read book | Audience: Grades
    K-1 | Summary: "Describes what we can do to be kind to ourselves, such as taking care of our bodies, being
    aware of our thoughts, and looking for helpers when we need them. An early social-emotional learning
    book that includes a note to caregivers, reading activities, and a word list" — Provided by publisher.
Identifiers: LCCN 2019048907 (print) | LCCN 2019048908 (ebook) | ISBN 9781684508938 (hardcover) |
    ISBN 9781684045174 (paperback) | ISBN 9781684045211 (epub)
Subjects: LCSH: Self-esteem—Juvenile literature. | Self-care, Health—Juvenile literature.
Classification: LCC BF723.S3 L56 2021 (print) | LCC BF723.S3 (ebook) | DDC 646.70083/3—dc23
LC record available at https://lccn.loc.gov/2019048907
LC ebook record available at https://lccn.loc.gov/2019048908

Hardcover ISBN: 978-1-68450-893-8
Paperback ISBN: 978-1-68404-517-4

Everyone has good days.

And everyone
has bad days.

No matter what
kind of day
you're having,
you can choose
to be kind
to yourself.

You can be kind
to your body.

You can eat
healthy foods.

You can choose
to move sometimes.

You can choose
to rest sometimes.

And you can get
plenty of sleep.

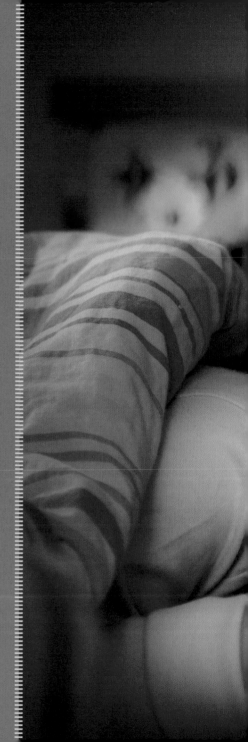

You can be kind
to yourself in
other ways, too.

You can choose
to do things
that make you
feel happy.

You can choose
to do things
that make you
feel calm.

You can choose
kind and helpful
words to say
to yourself.

You can think them.

You can say them.

You can even
write them.

You can find
people who are
kind and spend
time with them.

You can find
people who are
helpful and ask
them for help
when you need it.

You can always choose to be kind to yourself.

It doesn't matter where you are.

It doesn't matter
who you're with.

Being kind to
yourself makes
the bad days feel
not quite so bad.

And it makes
the good days
feel even better!

## CRAFT AND STRUCTURE

To check your child's understanding of the organization of the book, recreate the following chart on a sheet of paper. Ask your child to complete the chart by writing words or ideas from the text about ways to be kind to yourself.

| Your Body | Your Feelings | Kind Words | Kind People |
|---|---|---|---|
|  |  |  |  |

## VOCABULARY: Learning Content Words

Content words are words that are specific to a particular topic. All of the content words in this book can be found on page 32. Use some or all of these content words to complete one or more of the following activities:

• Help your child find word parts or smaller words within the content words.

• Take turns acting out the words and guessing which word is being acted out.

• Write a few words with the letters scrambled. Say the definition of a word and have your child unscramble the letters for the correct word.

• Write the compound words on slips of paper and cut them into their smaller parts. Mix them up and have your child match the shorter words to make each compound word.

• Give your child 3 to 4 clues about the meaning of a word and have him or her name the word being defined.

## FOUNDATIONAL SKILLS: Word Endings

*Word endings* are letters or groups of letters added to the end of a word to change its meaning or to form a different word. Have your child identify the word endings in the list of words below. Then help your child find words with word endings in this book.

| horses | flying | played |
| hopeful | timeless | likeable |

## CLOSE READING OF INFORMATIONAL TEXT

Close reading helps children comprehend text. It includes reading a text, discussing it with others, and answering questions about it. Use these questions to discuss this book with your child:

• Why is it important to be kind to yourself?

• What is something you do to be kind to yourself?

• How is eating healthy foods being kind to yourself?

• When is it a good time to be kind to yourself?

• Why is asking for help being kind to yourself?

• How does being kind to yourself affect your day?

## FLUENCY

Fluency is the ability to read accurately with speed and expression. Help your child practice fluency by using one or more of the following activities:

• Reread the book to your child at least two times while he or she uses a finger to track each word as it is read.

• Read a line of the book, then reread it as your child reads along with you.

• Ask your child to go back through the book and read the words he or she knows.

• Have your child practice reading the book several times to improve accuracy, rate, and expression.

# ••• Word List •••

*Being Kind to Yourself* uses the 68 words listed below. *High-frequency words* are those words that are used most often in the English language. They are sometimes referred to as *sight words* because children need to learn to recognize them automatically when they read. *Content words* are any words specific to a particular topic. Regular practice reading these words will enhance your child's ability to read with greater fluency and comprehension.

## High-Frequency Words

| | | | | |
|---|---|---|---|---|
| always | even | it | that | what |
| and | find | make(s) | the | when |
| are | for | no | them | where |
| ask | get | not | things | who |
| be(ing) | good | of | think | with |
| can | has | other | time | word(s) |
| day(s) | have(ing) | people | to | write |
| do | help(ful) | say | too | you |
| eat | in | so | way(s) | your |

## Content Words

| | | | | |
|---|---|---|---|---|
| bad | doesn't | healthy | plenty | spend |
| better | everyone | kind | quite | you're |
| body | feel | matter | rest | yourself |
| calm | foods | move | sleep | |
| choose | happy | need | sometimes | |

### ••• About the Author

Mary Lindeen is a writer, editor, parent, and former elementary school teacher. She has written more than 100 books for children and edited many more. She specializes in early literacy instruction and books for young readers, especially nonfiction.